The
POWER
Of
Thanksgiving
a 90-Day Devotional

Omotoke O. Oloruntoba

ISBN-13: 978-0-9991190-0-6
ISBN-10: 0-9991190-0-1

Introduction

This devotional was created for your daily use and the transformation of your life. How do I know? When I birthed this book, I was on an assignment to praise God for 90 days for what he was getting ready to do in my life not really knowing the magnitude of what he was getting ready to do. I have been on this journey and I know first-hand what lies at the end. Guess what happened, on exactly Day 90? I experienced a great breakthrough.

As you navigate this book daily, engage with God will all your heart and be clear in your heart about the change you want to see. I guarantee you a few things will happen:

1) The way you appreciate God will change for the better.
2) You will see things start to take shape.
3) Joy will become your daily portion.

I want you to view thanksgiving as a weapon throughout this journey. I made it simple; three points of thanksgiving daily for the next 90 days to appreciate the one who is the creator of the heaven and the earth, who makes all things possible and beautiful in his own time. Through the use of this systematic approach, not only are you appreciating him, you are speaking to him according to his own words. I need you to speak out loud the word of God and watch it not return back void. Read, give thanks to God daily for the next 90 days, then make it a lifestyle. Discover the power of Thanksgiving.

Much Love,
Omotoke Oloruntoba

Dedication

I dedicate this book first and foremost to Jesus Christ, my lord and savior, the lover of my soul, the ruler of my life, the pillar that holds and anchors me, my rock and my salvation. Lord, I thank you for being who you say you are!

I dedicate this book to my parents, Abdul and Ngozi Oloruntoba for loving me unconditionally, never giving up on me when you had every reason to and for labouring for me constantly in the place of prayer. I love you.

I dedicate this book to my spiritual parents, Apostle and Lady Apostle Bassey for their great mentorship and genuine love for the body of Christ.

I dedicate this book to Deacon Touch and Pastor Favour Malefo for their incredible love, support and exemplary leadership.

I dedicate this book to Prophet John Enumah for the inspiration and letting God use him as his oracle.

I dedicate this book to Olufemi Oloyede for his consistent support and encouragement.

I dedicate this book to every worshipper, those who give thanks to the Lord constantly with oneness of heart. You will indeed reap the fruits of your Praises!

Foreword

This devotional is effective and profitable for daily living; it will lead you to discover the purpose and **effects** of thanksgiving. Yes, this manual was created for you to see RESULTS! In the bible, David acknowledged the importance of Thanksgiving as stated in Psalm 92 vs 1-3 *"It is a good thing to give thanks unto the Lord, and to sing praises unto thy name, O Most High: To shew forth thy lovingkindness in the morning, and thy faithfulness every night,*
Upon an instrument of ten strings, and upon the psaltery; upon the harp with a solemn sound".

What many people have not come to realize is that there are many blessings that come from being grateful for the good things we already have. Being grateful makes you happier and healthier and it also provokes the heavens to act on your behalf speedily. Did you know that literally counting your blessings increases your emotional health? How do I know? Do you know any happy person who is not grateful or grateful person who isn't happy?

A grateful heart is a receiving heart. When you are thankful for little things, you will soon start to notice bigger things coming your way. When we thank God for anything he does, he is ready to do more for us. Furthermore, when we thank God for that which is has not done yet, it provokes his hand to move on our behalf.

Keep in mind, another way to show appreciation is living a lifestyle that is acceptable and pleasing to God, by making the death of Jesus of importance and of value. Jesus paid the ultimate price for us, to show the heart of gratitude, we must forsake our sinful ways and embrace righteousness. God is not interested in what we bring, or how we give thanks, but he is interested in the individual that is rendering thanks. You must be in tune with God before

your thanksgiving can be accepted and if your thanksgiving is accepted, only then can the principle of "Open Heavens through thanksgiving" work for you.

This book enables you to apply this great spiritual principle! Thanksgiving and praise to God literally opens the barriers that separate the realms of Heaven from the realms of the earth and allows people to move into the presence of the Lord because he inhabits the praises and thanks of his people. Start this exercise and find out!

Olufemi Oloyede

Day 1

Psalm 3:3 But Thou, O Lord, art a shield for me; My glory, and the lifter of my head.

- Lord, I thank you for being my glory.
- Thank you for being the lifter of my head.
- Lord, I thank you because of this, I will not be put to shame.

Day 2

Psalm 44:8 In God we boast all day long and praise thy name forever. Selah.

- Lord, I thank you because I can boast in you and your mighty works.
- Thank you because I can boast in your consistency and dependability.
- Lord, I thank you because of your greatness, I can boldly show off your mighty works in my life.

Day 3

Psalm 34:4 I sought the Lord and he heard me, and delivered me from all my fears.

- Lord I thank you for being a prayer answering and consistent father.
- Thank you Lord because I can seek you and expect an answer.
- Lord, thank you for your willingness to respond to me when I seek your presence, guidance and help.

Day 4

Matthew 7:7 Ask, and it shall be given you, seek, and ye shall find, knock, and it shall be opened unto you.

- Lord, I thank you that your word is true.
- Thank you Lord because I will ask and it shall be given to me by faith in Jesus name.
- Lord, I thank you for opening doors of success for me upon my request.

Day 5

Isaiah 40:28 Hast thou not known? Hast thou not heard, that the everlasting God, the Lord, the Creator of the ends of the earth, fainteth not, neither is weary? There is no searching his understanding.

- Lord, I thank you for your character.
- I thank you Lord because you do not get weary or tired.
- Lord, I thank you for constantly moving on my behalf.

Day 6

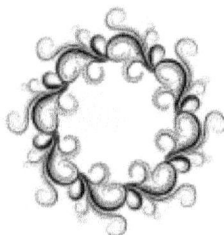

Psalm 46:1 God is our refuge and strength. An ever -present help in the time of trouble.

- Lord, I thank you for always being there whenever I desperately need you.
- Thank you Lord for being my refuge and a shelter from danger and difficulty.
- Lord I thank you for being my strength and stepping up in times of my weakness.

Day 7

Psalm 81:10b Open your mouth wide and I will fill it.

- Lord, I thank you because I know my mouth will be filled with testimonies of how you made a way for me.
- Thank you Lord because you will fill my mouth with good news.
- Lord, I thank you because my mouth will also be filled with words of encouragement for others as I testify of your goodness.

Day 8

Isaiah 55:12 For ye shall go out with joy and be led forth in peace.

- Lord, I thank you for joy unspeakable, the kind of joy that no one can explain.
- Thank you Lord for your peace that passes all understanding despite the circumstances that may surround me.
- Lord I thank you because you will lead me in that peace for the rest of my life.

Day 9

Hebrew 13:8 Jesus Christ the same today, yesterday and forever.

- Lord, I thank you because you are the unchangeable changer.
- Thank you Lord because you remain the same but you are able to change any and all situations.
- Lord I acknowledge and appreciate your consistency in my life.

Day 10

Psalm 37:25 I have been young, now am old yet have I not seen the righteous forsaken, nor his seed begging bread.

- Lord, I thank you for surplus, for supplying me with more than I need.
- Thank you Lord for the fact that you will never forsake me because through your son Jesus I have been made righteous.
- Lord, I thank you because those that you love will never be put to shame.

Day 11

Romans 8:28 And we know that all things worketh together for good to them that love God and are called according to his purpose.

- Lord, I thank you because according to your word you are working ALL things out for my good.
- Thank you for perfecting all that concerns me in the midst of trials and temptations.
- Lord, I thank you because even the events of my life that may cause dissatisfaction will eventually lead to victory.

Day 12

Psalm 37:23a The steps of a good man are ordered by the Lord.

- Lord, I thank you because I know you are ordering all my steps.
- Thank you for connecting me to the right people in order to fulfill your ordained purpose and destiny of my life.
- Lord, I thank you for leading me to make the right decisions through your wisdom.

Day 13

Psalm 117:2 for his merciful kindness is great toward us: and the truth of the Lord endureth forever. Praise ye the Lord.

- Lord, I thank you for your never-ending mercies.
- Thank you lord because your mercies are new every morning; daily being refreshed so you can bestow it upon my life
- Lord, thank you because your truths concerning my life and my progress are forever and will surely come to pass!

Day 14

Proverbs 10:22 The blessing of the lord, it maketh rich and he addeth no sorrow with it.

- Lord, I thank you for riches in wealth, riches in peace, riches in progression and all the other riches you have bestowed upon me!
- I thank you because everything you bestow upon me adds no sorrow to it
- Lord, I thank you for the flow of all your blessings over my life.

Day 15

Isaiah 55:12 for ye shall go out with joy and be led forth in peace.

- Lord, I thank you for joy unspeakable; the type of joy that cannot simply be put into words
- Thank you lord for your peace that passeth all understanding in every area of my life.
- Lord, I thank you because the joy and peace you give is not determined by circumstances and situations and in spite of the things that surround me I still enjoy your peace.

Day 16

Psalm 127:1 Except the lord build the house, they labor in vain that build it.

- Lord, I thank you because I know my labor and efforts will not be in vain.
- Thank you Lord in advance that you will build and establish my house in Jesus name.
- Lord I thank you for strategically leading me to a life of effectiveness and not one of wasted attempts.

Day 17

Psalm 16:6 the lines are fallen unto me in pleasant places. Yea, I have a goodly heritage.

- Lord, I thank you for making everything fall in line in my life so beautifully!
- Thank you Lord in advance for aligning my life according to your good will for me
- Lord I thank you for giving me a good legacy by adopting me into the family of Jesus therefore making me heir to your kingdom.

Day 18

Psalm 71:5 thou art my hope o Lord God. Thou art my trust from my youth!

- Lord, I thank you for being my everlasting hope when I feel like giving up on everything
- Thank you Lord for being trustworthy and reliable.
- Thank you Lord for the longevity of your dependability. You have been by my side for as long as I can remember and continuously will be.

Day 19

Psalm 71:21 Thou shall increase my greatness and comfort me on every side.

- Lord I thank you for increase in greatness and continuous. progression in all areas of my life
- Thank you Lord for moving me into a new dimension materially and spiritually.
- Lord, I thank you for your comfort that is all around me in the midst of every and any situation.

Day 20

Psalm 100:5 For the lord is good. His mercy is everlasting and his truth endureth to all generations.

- Lord, I thank you for your goodness to me.
- Thank you for your continuous mercy over my life even when I did not deserve it.
- Lord, I thank you because your truth concerning my life (success, prosperity, etc.) is everlasting and will therefore manifest itself.

Day 21

Psalm 102:12 But thou, O Lord, shall endure forever and thy remembrance unto all generations.

- Lord, I thank you for your sovereignty and your reign over my life
- Thank you Lord for your kingdom shall endure forever
- Lord I thank you because the generations after me will know and remember you as their God.

Day 22

Proverbs 17:1 Better is a dry morsel, and quietness therewith, than a house full of sacrifices with strife.

- Lord, I thank you in advance in faith that my house will be one of peace, joy and harmony in Jesus name.
- Thank you Lord because you are perfecting all that concerns my current and future home.
- Lord I thank you because I will have a home void of constant strife.

Day 23

Proverbs 18:10. The name of the Lord is a strong tower, the righteous run into it and are safe.

- Lord, I thank you for the strength of your name
- Thank you Lord because your name is distinguished from any other name like a tower is distinguished from a building!
- Lord I thank you because your name ensures safety on every side and safety in all difficult situations.

Day 24

Psalm 20:5 We will rejoice in thy salvation, and in the name of our God we will set up our banners: the LORD fulfill all thy petitions!

- Lord, I thank you in advance for fulfilling all my petitions and my cries to heaven.
- Thank you Lord for continuously giving me reasons to rejoice in your name.
- Lord, I thank you because your name is my banner and a true representation of an overflow of blessings over my life.

Day 25

Psalm 102:13 Thou shalt arise, and have mercy upon Zion: for the time to favor her, yea, the set time, is come.

- Lord, I thank you because my set and appointed time has come!
- Thank you Lord for the time for favor and settlement is here in Jesus name.
- Lord, I thank you for arising mightily on my behalf and showing your great mercy.

Day 26

Psalm 102:27 But thou art the same, and thy years shall have no end.

- Lord, I thank you because you remain the same in everything and all situations. Never changing and never wavering.
- Thank you Lord because that which you have done before you can and will surely do again.
- Lord I thank you for your everlasting reign in my life which shall know no end.

Day 27

Psalm 91:3 Surely he shall deliver thee from the snare of the fowler, and from the noisome pestilence.

- Lord, I thank you for delivering me from every snare and every deceit.
- Thank you Lord for exposing every plan of the enemy to trap me
- Lord, I thank you for your hand of protection that covers me and rescues me.

Day 28

Psalm 66:12 we went through fire and through water: but thou broughtest us out into a wealthy place.

- Lord, I thank you for bringing me through fire and water unharmed
- Thank you Lord because the test and trials are over
- Lord, I thank you because you are bringing me into a place of abundance! Abundant joy, peace, and unity in Jesus name!

Day 29

Psalm 46:5 God is in the midst of her; she shall not be moved: God shall help her, and that right early.

- Lord, I thank you for continuously being with me, fellowshipping with me constantly
- Thank you Lord for making me stable and unmovable despite the many storms and floods I have passed through
- Lord, I thank you for your constant helping hand.

Day 30

Exodus 14:14. The Lord shall fight for you and you shall hold your peace.

- Lord, I thank you for fighting many battles on my behalf both those that I am aware of as well as those that I am unaware of.
- Thank you because I can rest in the fact that you are avenging my case even without any effort on my part
- Thank you Lord for restoring my peace to me on every side.

It's been 30 days. How are you feeling? What are you feeling?
Are you connecting with God?
Don't get tired, keep on thanking him! Stay consistent. You will see results!

Day 31

Psalm 116:1-2 I love the LORD, because he hath heard my voice and my supplications. Because he hath inclined his ear unto me, therefore will I call upon him as long as I live.

- Lord, I thank you for inclining your ears unto me; hearing me whenever I call upon your name.
- Thank you Lord because your ears are not deaf towards my cries and supplications
- Lord, I thank you because I can recollect the countless times in which you have given me what my heart desires

Day 32

Psalm 116:17 I will offer to thee the sacrifice of thanksgiving, and will call upon the name of the LORD!

- Lord, I offer you the sacrifice of the fruit of my lips!
- Thank you Lord for the privilege of being able to call on you at any point in time
- Lord, you are more than worthy of my sacrifice of praise for everything you are doing, for what you have already done and for all you are getting ready to do.

Day 33

Psalm 149:4 For the LORD taketh pleasure in his people: he will beautify the meek with salvation.

- Lord, I thank you for beautifying my life with salvation.
- Thank you lord for saving me from the hands of wrong relationships, wrong friendships and destiny altering choices.
- Lord I thank you for the grace to do your good will and continuously taking pleasure in me.

Day 34

Daniel 4:3 How great are his signs! and how mighty are his wonders! his kingdom is an everlasting kingdom, and his dominion is from generation to generation.

- Lord I thank you for your signs and wonders in my life
- Thank you Lord for showcasing your greatness through my life
- Lord, thank you for your mighty works; your kingdom is everlasting!

Day 35

Psalm 18:2 The LORD is my rock, and my fortress, and my deliverer; my God, my strength, in whom I will trust; my buckler, and the horn of my salvation, and my high tower.

- Lord, I thank you because I can put my full trust in you!
- Thank you Lord for being a shield, a buckler, trustworthy, my rock, my salivation!
- Lord, I thank you because as I know that as I trust you for many things in faith, I will begin to see the manifestation in the name of Jesus.

Day 36

James 1: 17 Every good gift and every perfect gift is from above, and cometh down from the Father of lights, with whom is no variableness, neither shadow of turning.

- Lord I thank you for every good and perfect gift that you have bestowed upon me.
- Thank you Lord for helping me to put every gift to good use and serve in purpose
- Lord I thank you for using me to accomplish your will and teaching me how to steward that which you have given unto me.

Day 37

Psalm 145:18-19 The Lord is near to all who call on him, to all who call on him in truth. He will fulfill the desire of them that fear him: he also will hear their cry, and will save them.

- Lord, I thank you for being so near to me when I call upon you
- Thank you Lord for fulfilling the desires of my heart
- Lord, I thank you for hearing my cry and saving me from my despair and sorrow.

Day 38

Isaiah 50:7 For the Lord GOD will help me; therefore, shall I not be confounded: therefore, have I set my face like a flint, and I know that I shall not be ashamed.

- Lord, I thank you for I know you WILL help me in every area and aspect of my life!
- Thank you Lord because I will not be confused or bewildered by any circumstances that I face
- Lord, I thank you for ensuring that I will not be put to shame.

Day 39

Psalm 3:5 I laid me down and slept; I awaked; for the LORD sustained me.

- Lord, I thank you for allowing me to lie down to sleep and waking up unharmed but revived and refreshed
- Thank you Lord for your sustenance in all areas of my life.
- Lord, I thank you for allowing your keeping and sustaining power to work on my behalf.

Day 40

Isaiah 30:21 21 And thine ears shall hear a word behind thee, saying, this is the way, walk ye in it, when ye turn to the right hand, and when ye turn to the left.

- Lord, I thank you for the privilege of being able to hear from you concerning all areas of my life
- Thank you for giving me your divine direction that leads to your goodness
- Lord, I thank you because your word will continually lead me in the right direction.

Day 41

Psalm 44:3 3 For they got not the land in possession by their own sword, neither did their own arm save them: but thy right hand, and thine arm, and the light of thy countenance, because thou hadst a favor unto them.

- Lord, I thank you and acknowledge the fact that I am limited in my ability to accomplish anything on my own
- Thank you Lord, because I do not have to rely on my own strength.
- Lord, I thank you for your right hand that does not cease to work on my behalf.

Day 42

Psalm 6:9 The LORD hath heard my supplication; the LORD will receive my prayer.

- Lord, I thank you because I have confidence that you have heard my supplication.
- Thank you lord for receiving my prayers and giving them consideration.
- Lord, I thank you because I can come boldly to your throne of grace because I am sure you will hear me.

Day 43

Psalm 20:6 Now know I that the LORD saveth his anointed; he will hear him from his holy heaven with the saving strength of his right hand.

- Lord, I thank you always coming to my rescue because I belong to you
- Thank you Lord, for hearing me when I call on you from the heavens where you sit high and look low
- Lord I thank you for your right hand that continues to reach me and save me.

Day 44

Psalm 45:17 I will make thy name to be remembered in all generations: therefore, shall the people praise thee for ever and ever.

- Lord, I thank you for all of your promises concerning my life.
- Thank you Lord for my life shall be a testimony to all generations.
- Lord I thank you because my name shall be remembered by all people because of your favor upon my life.

Day 45

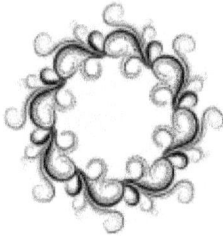

Psalm 75:6-7 For promotion cometh neither from the east, nor from the west, nor from the south but God is the judge: he putteth down one, and setteth up another.

- Lord, I thank you because you are the one true and living GOD; the one who has the ability to lift up and cast down.
- Thank you Lord for consistently and progressively promoting me
- Lord, thank you for elevation in every area of my life.

Day 46

Psalm 103:13 Like as a father pitieth his children, so the LORD pitieth them that fear him.

- Lord, I thank you for showing your mercy upon my life and pitying me.
- Thank you Lord for your compassion concerning every affair of my life.
- Lord, I thank you because I know that your mercy will continue to work for me in Jesus name!

Day 47

Proverbs 3:26 For the LORD shall be thy confidence, and shall keep thy foot from being taken.

- Lord, I thank you for being my confidence!
- Thank you lord, for I know that My foot will never be trapped or taken by the snares of deceivers.
- Lord, I thank you because of my trust and confidence in you, I can move forward in boldness.

Day 48

Proverbs 3:24 When thou liest down, thou shalt not be afraid: yea, thou shalt lie down, and thy sleep shall be sweet.

- Lord, I thank you for removing every type of fears from my life; the fear of failure, fear of the unknown, fear of the future and all fears of life.
- Thank you Lord, for when I lay down to sleep, it shall be sweet.
- Lord I thank you because I will not be troubled by the affairs of life in Jesus name.

Day 49

Psalm 16:4 The lord is the portion of mine inheritance and of my cup: thou maintainest my lot.

- Lord, I thank you for being my portion; for you are mine and I am yours
- Thank you Lord, because in you I am complete
- Lord, I thank you for maintaining and sustaining every aspect and area of my life; My career, my finances, my marital destiny and every other area are in your hands and I know you will maintain and sustain them.

Day 50

Isaiah 33:10 Now will I rise, saith the LORD; now will I be exalted; now will I lift up myself.

- Lord, I thank you for arising to action on my behalf to judge every negative situation.
- Thank you Lord for exalting yourself over my case and everything that concerns me.
- Lord, I thank you because you are God all by yourself; with no help or assistance you will surely arise.

Day 51

Hebrew 2:8 Thou hast put all things in subjection under his feet. For in that he put all in subjection under him, he left nothing that is not put under him. But now we see not yet all things put under him.

- Lord, I thank you for all things which are under my subjection.
- Thank you Lord because of the authority I have through the name of Jesus
- Lord, I thank you because every situation is coming under the subjection of everything written in your word in Jesus name.

Day 52

Isaiah 40:31 But they that wait upon the LORD shall renew their strength; they shall mount up with wings as eagles; they shall run, and not be weary; and they shall walk, and not faint.

- Lord, I thank you for the continuous renewal of my strength.
- Thank you Lord for not allowing me to faint in the midst of trials and storms of life
- Lord, I thank you for giving me the ability to run this race and not be weary.

Day 53

Isaiah 40:5 And the glory of the LORD shall be revealed, and all flesh shall see it together: for the mouth of the LORD hath spoken it.

- Lord, I thank you because your glory will surely be revealed in my life
- Thank you Lord for continuously using my life as a platform to showcase your glory for all to see
- Lord, I thank you because whatsoever you have spoken, I will see it come to pass in my life in Jesus name.

Day 54

Psalm 63:3-4 because thy loving kindness is better than life, my lips shall praise thee. Thus will I bless thee while I live: I will lift up my hands in thy name.

- Lord, I thank you for your loving kindness that I experience each and every day.
- Thank you Lord, for your kindness is better than anything I can ever imagine
- Lord I thank you for giving me the grace to lift up my hands in surrender to your sovereignty over my life.

Day 55

Psalm 54: 4 Behold, God is mine helper: The Lord is with them that uphold my soul.

- Lord I thank for being my helper and continuously upholding my soul.
- Thank you being an ever-present help in the time of need.
- Lord, I thank you for your hand upon my life that preserves me.

Day 56

Psalm 57:2 2 I will cry unto God most high; unto God that performeth all things for me.

- Lord, I thank you because I can cry out my soul to you with the assurance that you will answer.
- Thank you Lord for performing continuously for me and through me.
- Lord, I thank you because your hand is never resting on my behalf and for this I give you all honor and adoration.

Day 57

Psalm 148:13 Let them praise the name of the LORD: for his name alone is excellent; his glory is above the earth and heaven.

- Lord I thank you for your name is indeed excellent; you are perfect in all your ways!
- Thank you for being the sovereign king who is above the heaven and the earth
- Lord, I thank you for showing forth your glory through your creations.

Day 58

Psalm 147:5 Great is our Lord, and of great power: his understanding is infinite.

- Lord, I thank you for your greatness and your great power; your power is unmatched.
- Thank you lord for your understanding and your unfathomable wisdom. Your ways are not our ways neither are your thoughts our thoughts.
- Lord, I thank you because of your wisdom I am rest assured that my life is in good hands.

Day 59

Romans 8:34 Who is he that condemneth? It is Christ that died, yea rather, that is risen again, who is even at the right hand of God, who also maketh intercession for us.

- Lord, I Thank you for our Lord Jesus Christ; who is consistently interceding and pleading on my behalf concerning all aspects of my life and welfare.
- Thank you Lord for your everlasting and deep love that is evident daily.
- Lord, I thank you for loving me unconditionally in spite of my many flaws

Day 60

Psalm 60:12 Through God we shall do valiantly: for it is he that shall tread down our enemies.

- Lord, I thank you for the spirit of courage and boldness through the Holy Spirit.
- Thank you Lord for giving me the ability to move like a valiant/brave soldier in battle.
- Lord, I thank you for fighting all my battles and crushing all enemies and allowing me to experience victory on every side.

It's been 60 days. Are you still thanking him with the same intensity as when you started? Do Not Get Weary! Push Through! You have so many reasons to be grateful. Focus and press in!

Day 61

Joel 2:26 And ye shall eat in plenty, and be satisfied, and praise the name of the LORD your God, that hath dealt wondrously with you: and my people shall never be ashamed.

- Lord, I thank you for allowing me to eat in plenty and be satisfied.
- Thank you Lord for your abundant provision and surplus in every area of my life.
- Lord, I thank you for dealing wondrously with me and wiping away every form of shame in my life.

Day 62

Joel 2:33 And it shall come to pass, that whosoever shall call on the name of the LORD shall be delivered: for in mount Zion and in Jerusalem shall be deliverance, as the LORD hath said, and in the remnant whom the LORD shall call.

- Lord, I thank you because whosoever calls upon your name shall/must be delivered.
- Thank you Lord, for your deliverance has been apportioned to me by reason of me calling upon your name.
- Lord, I thank you because your word concerning my life is true!

Day 63

Job 42:10 and the lord turned the captivity of Job, when he prayed for his friends: also the Lord gave Job twice as much as he had before.

- Lord, I Thank you because you are turning my captivity around like that of Job.
- Thank you Lord for the restoration of all lost time and efforts.
- Lord, I Thank you in advance for giving me twice as much as I have lost to your glory! Praises be to your name!

Day 64

Job 36:26 Behold, God is great, and we know him not, neither can the number of his years be searched out.

- Lord, I Thank you for your greatness and unfathomable nature
- Thank you Lord, for revealing more and more of yourself to me; you are so great there is so much more of you to experience
- Lord, I thank you for the privilege of knowing you and for showing the wonderful works you are capable of.

Day 65

Psalm 77:1 I cried unto God with my voice, even unto God with my voice; and he gave ear unto me.

- Lord, I thank you because your ears are inclined to the petitions of my heart.
- Thank you Lord, for I know that my tears are not in vain and you have heard and seen them as you saw Hannah when she cried out and poured out her soul unto you
- Lord, I thank you for showing compassion and graciousness towards my situation

Day 66

Job 4:8-9 I would seek unto God, and unto God would I commit my cause: Which doeth great things and unsearchable; marvelous things without number.

- Lord, I thank you for being able to commit my cause unto you. Lord, you are dependable!
- Thank you Lord for the marvelous things you are able to do in my life.
- Lord, I thank you for the great things that you are currently doing as I wait for your manifestation in Jesus name.

Day 67

Psalm 109:21 But do thou for me, O GOD the Lord, for thy name's sake: because thy mercy is good, deliver thou me.

- Lord, I thank you for because for your namesake you will do according to your promises concerning my life.
- Thank you Lord for your mercy will continue to speak in my life.
- Lord, I thank you for I know that you will deliver me from every shame and reproach in Jesus name.

Day 68

Exodus 33:17 And the LORD said unto Moses, I will do this thing also that thou hast spoken: for thou hast found grace in my sight, and I know thee by name.

- Lord, I thank you because that which I have declared and spoken concerning my life will surely come to pass according to your word.
- Thank you Lord because I can already see the manifestation of things to come.
- Lord, I thank you the grace and mercy I have found in your sight.

Day 69

Psalm 80:19 Turn us again, O LORD God of hosts, cause thy face to shine; and we shall be saved.

- Lord, I thank you for restoration!
- Thank you Lord for turning me again to my rightful place and position in life.
- Lord, I thank you for causing your face to shine upon me and for saving me from every mistake and all destruction.

Day 70

**Psalm 46:7 The LORD of hosts is with us;
the God of Jacob is our refuge. Selah.**

- Lord, I thank you for being present
  with me in all situations.
- Thank you Lord for being my refuge
  and shelter indeed.
- Lord, I thank you because I can rely
  on you for your security and safety.

Day 71

Psalm 85:8a I will hear what God the LORD will speak: for he will speak peace unto his people, and to his saints.

- Lord, I thank you for speaking your peace to me!
- Thank you Lord because your peace that passeth all understanding will rule in my heart.
- Lord, I thank you because your peace will lead and guide me into your perfect will in Jesus name.

Day 72

Psalm 105:43-44 And he brought forth his people with joy, and his chosen with gladness: And gave them the lands of the heathen: and they inherited the labor of the people.

- Lord, I thank you for giving me your oil of joy and gladness.
- Thank you Lord for giving me grace to possess my possessions in the land that I dwell.
- Lord, I thank you for the reward for the labor of my own and that of others.

Day 73

Jeremiah 33:6 Behold, I will bring it health and cure, and I will cure them, and will reveal unto them the abundance of peace and truth.

- Lord, I thank you for your healing and restoration of health to my heart and soul.
- Thank you lord for you will continue to reveal to me in abundance your peace and your truth.
- Lord, I thank you because I believe that I will experience this peace and truth in a way I have never experienced it before.

Day 74

I Samuel 2:1 And Hannah prayed, and said, my heart rejoiceth in the LORD, mine horn is exalted in the LORD: my mouth is enlarged over mine enemies; because I rejoice in thy salvation.

- Lord, I thank you for causing my heart to rejoice in you and your mighty works.
- Thank you Lord for continuing to exalt and elevate me in all aspects of my life.
- Lord, I thank you for enlarging me beyond my imagination.

Day 75

Psalm 91:1 He that dwelleth in the secret place of the most High shall abide under the shadow of the Almighty.

- Lord, I Thank God for allowing me to dwell in your secret place and enjoy your rest.
- Thank you Lord because abiding in you ensures my security and safety.
- Lord, I thank you for continuing to preserve and shield me.

Day 76

Psalm 89:1 I will sing of the mercies of the LORD forever: with my mouth will I make known thy faithfulness to all generations.

- Lord, I thank you for your mercies are new every morning.
- Thank you Lord for the ability to recognize your works and give you the glory.
- Lord, I thank you for your faithfulness in my life that causes others to wonder what the secret is.

Day 77

I Peter 5:10-11 But the God of all grace, who hath called us unto his eternal glory by Christ Jesus, after ye have suffered a while, make you perfect, establish, strengthen, settle you. To him be glory and dominion for ever and ever.

- Lord, I thank you for your grace that is ever sufficient to withstand trials and temptations
- Thank you Lord because this is my season of perfection, establishment and settlement.
- Lord, I thank you for your finished work in my life.

Day 78

Isaiah 60:2 For, behold, the darkness shall cover the earth, and gross darkness the people: but the LORD shall arise upon thee, and his glory shall be seen upon thee.

- Lord, I thank you for singling me out and allowing your glory to shine upon me.
- Thank you Lord because despite what goes on around me your hand will continuously work for me.
- Lord, I thank you for I know you will continue to arise on my behalf in all situations.

Day 79

Psalm 84:11 For the LORD God is a sun and shield: the LORD will give grace and glory: no good thing will he withhold from them that walk uprightly.

- Lord, I thank you for being both a sun and a shield over my life and substance.
- Thank you Lord for your grace every day and your glory that continues to shine upon my life.
- Lord, I thank you because you will not withhold any good thing from me.

Day 80

Psalm 126:1-2 When the LORD turned again the captivity of Zion, we were like them that dream. Then was our mouth filled with laughter, and our tongue with singing: then said they among the heathen, The LORD hath done great things for them.

- Lord, I thank you for unexpected turnarounds getting ready to occur
- Thank you Lord for laughter and singing.
- Lord, I thank you for putting me on display!

Day 81

1 John 5: 14-15 And this is the confidence that we have in him, that, if we ask any thing according to his will, he heareth us: And if we know that he hear us, whatsoever we ask, we know that we have the petitions that we desired of him.

- Lord, I thank you because I can have confidence in you and your word!
- Thank you Lord for confidence that if I ask anything according to your will, you hear me!
- Lord, I thank you for fulfilling the desires of my heart. You are such an awesome God!

Day 82

Psalm 85:12 Yea, the LORD shall give that which is good; and our land shall yield her increase.

- Lord, I thank you because you indeed give gifts unto your children which are good! No good thing will you withhold from those who fear you!
- Thank you Lord because every perfect gift comes from You!
- Lord, I thank you because it is sure that I will experience increase on every side!

Day 83

Psalm 50:23 Whoso offereth praise glorifieth me: and to him that ordereth his conversation aright will I shew the salvation of God.

- Lord, I thank you for I know my praises shall reach the heavens and glorify you. You are worthy to be praised and adored.
- Thank you Lord for saving me and showing me the greatness of your salvation.
- Lord, I thank you for continuously saving me even when I am undeserving of it. Blessed be your holy name!

Day 84

Psalm 86:15 But thou, O Lord, art a God full of compassion, and gracious, longsuffering, and plenteous in mercy and truth.

- Lord, I thank you because you are a great father who is full of compassion.
- Thank you Lord for feeling my pain when we feel it and understanding my hurts.
- Lord, I thank you for being gracious, having abundant patience with me.

Day 85

Psalm 140:7 O GOD the Lord, the strength of my salvation, thou hast covered my head in the day of battle.

- Lord, I thank you for being my strength and shield!
- Thank you Lord for covering me from the target of my enemies.
- Lord, I thank you for your protection even in the midst of trouble.

Day 86

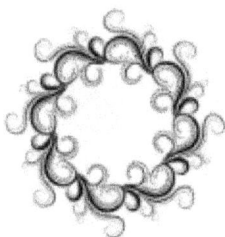

Proverbs 24:16 For a just man falleth seven times, and riseth up again: but the wicked shall fall into mischief.

- Lord, I thank you because you are always there to pick me up when I fall no matter how many times.
- Thank you Lord for your continuous grace and mercy.
- Lord, I thank you because as I rise up every enemy of progress and breakthrough will fall in Jesus name.

Day 87

Joshua 1:9 Have not I commanded thee? Be strong and of a good courage; be not afraid, neither be thou dismayed: for the LORD thy God is with thee whithersoever thou goest.

- Lord, I thank you for your never-ending presence that keeps me strong and gives me courage!
- Thank you Lord for removing every fear of the unknown from my heart.
- Lord, I thank you for being with me wherever I go.

Day 88

Isaiah 55:13 Instead of the thorn shall come up the fir tree, and instead of the brier shall come up the myrtle tree: and it shall be to the LORD for a name, for an everlasting sign that shall not be cut off.

- Lord, I thank you because every thorn is being removed from my life and the fir tree which brings fruits is coming up!
- Thank you Lord for uprooting from my life every unproductive thing.
- Lord, I thank you for making sure the evidence of your continuous work in my life is seen!

Day 89

Psalm 35:9-10. And my soul shall be joyful in the LORD: it shall rejoice in his salvation. All my bones shall say, LORD, who is like unto thee, which deliverest the poor from him that is too strong for him, yea, the poor and the needy from him that spoileth him.

- Lord, I thank you for your unspeakable joy!
- Thank you Lord because you are unmatchable! There is no one like You!
- Lord, I thank you for deliverance from every situation that is beyond my strength.

Day 90

I Kings 8:56 Blessed be the LORD, that hath given rest unto his people Israel, according to all that he promised: there hath not failed one word of all his good promise, which he promised by the hand of Moses his servant.

- Lord, I thank you for giving me rest on every side!
- Thank you Lord for doing according to ALL that you have promised!
- Lord, I thank you because your words to me have NOT failed, neither will they ever fail.

Lord, I thank you for the past 90 days and the fruitfulness of this season! Thank you Lord for taking me into a new dimension of praise and thanksgiving! Glory be unto your mighty name!

You made it! 90 days of Praising God! Why? Because he is truly worthy of your praise! Please share your testimonies and great news with us via email! We want to hear what God did for you in 90 days because others can be encouraged by your breakthrough!

Author Info

Omotoke Oloruntoba, is a woman who has a passion about God and his kingdom. Her passion for the body of Christ gives her the burden to constantly liberate individuals through deep revelations of the word of God. She is a first time author, founder & CEO of LGE Group, a firm that is a conglomerate with organizations in several industries. She studied Business Management at Stony Brook University (Bachelor of Science) in New York and has over 5 years of experience in Finance and Leadership. She is currently a MBA Candidate at the University of Illinois - Urbana Champaign. She currently resides outside of London, in the United Kingdom and hopes to continue to spread the good news of God's love and equip individuals on how to live a fruitful and effective life.

Contact:
Omotoke Oloruntoba
Email: ooloruntoba@LGEGroups.com
Website: www.LGEGroups.com